A million candles have burned
themselves out.   Still I read on.
—Montresor.

A McGRAW-HILL NEW BIOLOGY

Scientific Adviser: Dr. Gwynne Vevers

BEES & WASPS

A McGRAW-HILL NEW BIOLOGY

J. L. Cloudsley-Thompson

Bees & Wasps

Illustrated by Joyce Bee

McGRAW-HILL BOOK COMPANY

New York   San Francisco

Library of Congress Cataloging in Publication Data

Cloudsley-Thompson, J. L.
Bees & wasps.

(A McGraw-Hill new biology)
Includes index.
SUMMARY: Introduces the physical characteristics,
habits, and habitat of bees and wasps.
1. Bees—Juvenile literature. 2. Wasps—Juvenile
literature. I. Bee, Joyce. II. Title.
QL565.2.C56   595.7′99   75-26978
ISBN 0-07-064461-6 lib. bdg.

BEES & WASPS
First distribution in the United States of America
by McGraw-Hill Book Company, 1976.
Text © J. L. Cloudsley-Thompson 1974.
Illustrations © Joyce Bee 1974.
First printed in Great Britain for
The Bodley Head
by William Clowes & Sons Ltd., Beccles
First published 1974

Contents

Honeybee

Worker

Drone

Queen

Bumblebee

Cuckoo Bee

Worker

Queen

Hornet

Wasp

Sand-wasp

All insects natural size

Bees and wasps. The hornet is a
very large species of social wasp.

1
Introduction

Bees and wasps are insects, but unlike most in-sects, several kinds of bees and wasps are "social," which means that the adults live long enough to be able to look after their young. A white butterfly lays her eggs on cabbage leaves, but she never sees the caterpillars into which they hatch. Although locusts migrate in dense swarms, they have nothing to do with their eggs after laying them. Insects which live together like this, but do not look after their young, are called "gregarious."

Most kinds of insects are either solitary and live alone, or they are gregarious. Aphids (or greenfly) are gregarious, as are cockroaches, grasshoppers, and many kinds of caterpillars. But only two "orders" (or groups) of insects are social. One contains the termites (or "white ants"), the other bees, wasps and true ants.

A few other orders include insects which are said to be "sub-social." Female earwigs, for instance, lay their eggs in holes that they have dug in the ground. The eggs are guarded until they hatch, and after-wards the mother looks after her babies for a day or two. Rove beetles behave in a rather similar way. The female excavates a chamber in a pat of cow dung and lays her eggs in it. She will defend them

Dung-beetles pushing their ball of dung.

against intruders, including the larger larvae of her own species. When the eggs hatch, the young larvae stay with their mother until just before their first moult.

Dung-beetles also behave like this. These insects act as scavengers by breaking up and burying the droppings of cattle and other animals. They make balls of the dung, and roll them away, pushing with their broad heads or pulling backwards with their legs. After burying a good store of this nutritious food, the female dung-beetle lays an egg in each of her dung balls. Then she guards them while the larvae are feeding and growing. When the young beetles emerge, she escorts them to the outside world and her little family disperses.

Insect behavior is instinctive. Insects cannot know what they are doing, or why. Their brains drive them like machines and they are not conscious of their behavior in the way that we are. Nevertheless, bees and wasps have an especially good memory and a sense of time. Their behavior is more complex and on a higher level than that of solitary or gregarious insects.

Whereas all female sub-social insects can be mothers, very few of the bees or wasps in a social colony lay eggs or have babies. Every social insect does a special job. The wasps and honeybees that you see flying around are "workers." Their task is to collect food, to nurse the young grubs, and so on. Egg-laying is the work of "queens" who seldom leave the nest. The queen stays at home in the nest or hive, laying eggs all the time. She is fed and looked after by the workers. Sub-social insects do not behave like this. They look after their young, but only for a short time. Then the family breaks up. In social insects the young stay with their mother and help to rear their younger brothers and sisters.

The eggs hatch into maggot-like grubs or "larvae," which are wingless and quite different from adult insects. These grubs feed, grow and then change into a resting stage or "pupa," from which the adult insect finally emerges. During this time they are living in "brood" cells (or six-sided compartments) made of wax, inside the nest or hive.

Some of these cells are used for storing honey, which is why men have for centuries built beehives to attract the bees to build their nests inside. The cells filled with honey make up the honeycombs which you can eat.

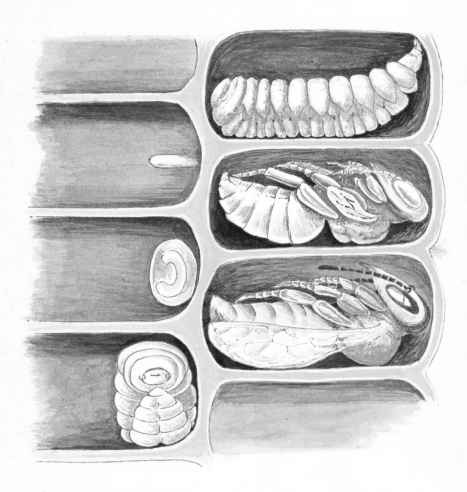

Stages in the development of the worker honeybee from the egg (top left) to the adult ready to emerge (bottom right). This takes about three weeks.

Worker honeybees exchanging food. The worker on the right is about to regurgitate a drop of food from her crop through her proboscis to the worker on the left who will suck it down her own proboscis.

Insect societies are overgrown families. All the 80,000 worker bees in a flourishing hive are daughters of the same queen. They are sisters, but they recognize one another only by the fact that members of the same colony smell alike.

Social insects are continually sharing their food. Bees feed on "nectar," a sweet liquid which they collect from flowers. Before a drop of nectar is finally digested, it will have passed many times from one bee to another. Mutual exchange of food is a bond which holds the colony together, and this is what makes the members of a colony all smell the same. They also exchange a substance which lets them know that the queen is alive and well.

2
Daily life in the beehive

Social insects are very busy creatures. In warm weather their day begins at sunrise and they do not rest until dusk. The life of a young worker bee is ordained from the moment that she emerges from the brood cell. At first, she works at cleaning other brood cells. These are the cells of the hive in which the eggs and grubs are developing. At the same time,

The workers attacking an intruder from another hive.

Workers cleaning open brood cells, removing rubbish left by previous occupants.

she helps to keep the brood warm. From the third day of adult life, the young worker begins to feed the older larvae. Later, she attends to the younger grubs and the queen.

After about two weeks of adult life, worker bees begin secreting wax, building honeycombs, and cleaning the hive. Then they spend a couple of days guarding the hive. Only bees that have the correct smell are allowed to enter. Members of other colonies are driven off or killed. The last three weeks of a honeybee's life are spent gathering food for the colony.

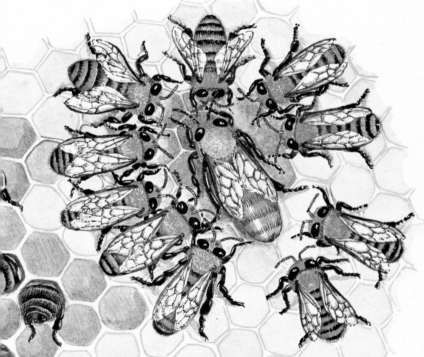

Workers licking the queen in the center of the group. This keeps her clean and at the same time the workers obtain the "queen substance" which they pass to other members of the hive so that they all know the queen is alive and well. If this stops, another queen is reared immediately (see p. 27).

13

Foraging honeybees collect and store a number of useful substances in their hives. Of these, the most important are nectar, pollen, and water. Nectar is collected from many different kinds of flowers and is stored as honey in the cells of the hive. Honeybees acquire their characteristic smells while visiting flowers. No two colonies will have received nectar from exactly the same flowers, so no two colonies smell exactly alike. In addition to nectar, bees also collect the juices of ripe fruit and other sweet liquids.

Worker bees tend to go to the same flowers at exactly the same time, day after day. They have a

Worker honeybees collecting nectar and pollen. The pollen baskets on the back legs of the two right-hand workers are full.

very accurate sense of time. This is important because some flowers, such as buckwheat, produce nectar mainly at a particular hour of the day. (Buckwheat is a cereal plant whose seed is used to make breakfast cakes and to feed horses and poultry.)

Pollen is nearly as important as nectar to bees. It is their only source of protein. The lives of worker bees are shortened if they do not eat pollen, and it is necessary for the development of the grubs. A little honey is added to the pollen when it is being stored for the winter. The mixture is called "bee-bread," and it keeps fresh for a long time.

15

Worker honeybee collecting gum from chestnut bud.

Worker bees collect gum or resin from the buds of various plants, especially trees. They use it as a kind of glue to fasten loose pieces of the comb and to fill up any cracks in the walls of the hive. It is also employed to varnish the insides of the cells before the queen places her eggs in them.

A bee sucks up nectar through her pointed "proboscis" and carries it away in her "crop" or "honey-stomach." Here the nectar is converted into honey by the action of salivary juices. It is easily regurgitated to feed other bees. If not used in this way, it is stored in the cells of the honeycomb. When a worker is gathering nectar, pollen tends to accumulate among the hairs with which her body is clothed. This is scraped off by stiff spines on the hind legs and stored in the "pollen baskets" above them on the outside of the legs. Then it is taken to the hive.

3
Comfort in the hive

Bees do not only suck up nectar. They also collect large amounts of water, especially when they live in hot climates. Some they use themselves, but the rest is brought back to the hive and regurgitated onto the combs so that it cools the hive by evaporation.

Worker honeybees collecting water.

Workers regularly ventilate their hive by fanning their wings at the entrances. This keeps the air inside cool and fresh. It also concentrates the nectar into honey by driving off excess water.

The hive is maintained at a very steady temperature, not much below that of our own bodies. In hot weather, it is cooled by fanning. In cold weather, it is warmed by the activities of the bees and their brood. The digestion of sugar automatically releases heat. In addition, when the temperature drops inside the hive, the worker bees become very active. They run about on the combs. This warms them up, because they use a lot of energy, and their bodies then heat the air in the hive. A single insect does not produce much heat but, when thousands of bees act together, they can keep their nest quite warm, even in the coldest winter.

Worker honeybees on the wooden entrance to the hive fanning air with their wings.

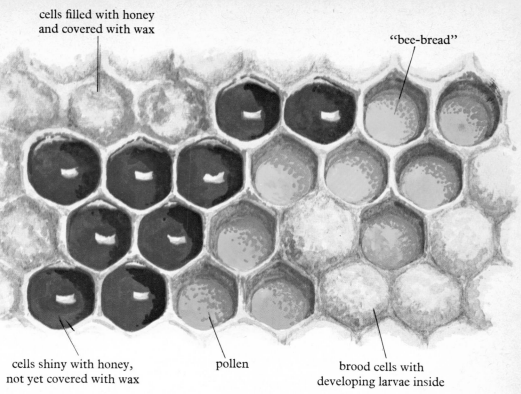

cells filled with honey
and covered with wax

"bee-bread"

cells shiny with honey,
not yet covered with wax

pollen

brood cells with
developing larvae inside

Larvae are rather sensitive to cooling, and the brood cells are always placed at the center of the hive, far from the entrance and from the outside walls. They spread through a number of combs. The honeycombs are built of bees' wax and arranged in parallel rows, like books on a shelf.

By combining together, social insects are able to maintain fairly constant temperatures in their nests. Like bees, social wasps also take water to their nests to cool the combs. In general, however, the temperatures of wasp nests are less uniform than those of honeybees. Bumblebees, whose colonies are very much smaller, have even less control of the temperature within their nests. Solitary bees and wasps have practically none.

4
The language of honeybees

Worker bees have glands at the ends of their abdomens. When bees are feeding on a rich source of food, these glands open and produce a scent which impregnates the food, helping other bees to find it.

On her return to the hive, a foraging bee dances, either at the entrance or on one of the combs. This dance tells the other workers where to look for nectar. When food is near, the forager does a "round" dance. She runs around in a circle, first one way, then the other. The bees close to her then leave the hive and set off to look for the food on which the dancing forager has left her scent. The richer the source of food, the more intense is the dancing and the larger the number of workers recruited.

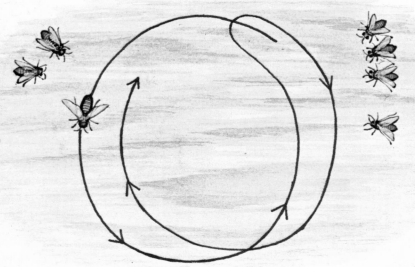

Diagram of the round dance at the wooden entrance to the hive.

If the source of food is further than about a hundred yards, the foraging worker does a "tail-wagging" dance on her return to the hive. She follows a "figure of eight" course on the comb. When she is on the straight part of her run, where the loops of the "eight" join, she "wags her tail." The number of tail-wags varies from two or three, when the source of food is about 130 yards off, to ten or eleven when it is over 800 yards away. In this manner, the dancing bee tells her sisters how far they will have to fly.

This is not all that a bee shows by her dance. She can also indicate the direction of a source of food. If she moves upwards when she is "wagging her tail,"

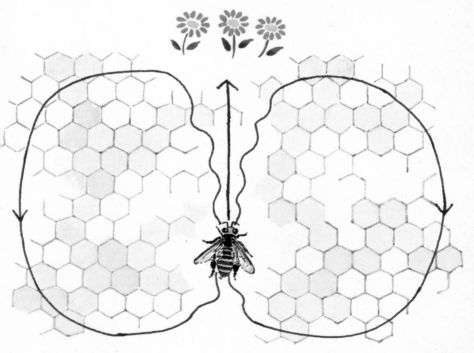

Diagram of the tail-wagging dance on the comb.

W.B.C. beehives (named after W. Broughton Carr, a distinguished British beekeeper) on heather moor. The bees build their combs vertically on wooden frames placed inside the hive. The entrance is at the bottom of the hive.

it means that the food lies towards the sun. If she moves downwards on the comb while "tail-wagging," the source of food must be directly away from the sun. Dancing bees also show if the food lies to the right or left of the sun's direction by the angle of their "tail-wagging" runs.

When the sun is obscured by clouds, worker bees respond to the direction of polarization of light in the sky. Our eyes are not sensitive to the plane of polarization of light, but the eyes of bees can respond to the direction in which the waves of light in blue sky are vibrating. That indicates where the sun lies, even when it cannot be seen.

The National beehive in a garden. The beekeeper can add extra frames if the bees find plenty of nectar.

If you find this difficult to understand, you may be quite sure that a bee cannot understand it either! She dances automatically, and her sister bees understand her dance instinctively.

Some people do not think that worker bees can convey all this information by their dances. They believe that bees must rely much more upon the sense of smell to find their way. Even if this is the case, however, bees are certainly able to pass messages in a remarkable way. For, as you must remember, their dances take place in pitch darkness and under very cramped conditions inside the hive.

5

Drones and the nuptial flight

Ordinary grubs in the brood cells of a beehive are fed mainly on honey and develop into worker bees. A few are given "royal jelly" which is secreted by glands that open into the mouths of the workers. These develop into queens. Queens are produced when a colony is preparing for swarming; and also if the old queen dies, or does not lay enough eggs. Both queens and workers develop from fertilized eggs. If the eggs are not fertilized, they produce males.

Worker bees are all females. Male bees are called "drones" and they do no work at all. Their only function is to fertilize the queens. Fertilization takes place in the air, and a swarm of drones follows the virgin queen as she flies upward from the hive. Only the fastest and strongest manages to catch her, and he always dies in the act of mating. This is because the male ejects sperm by generating such pressure in his abdomen that part of his reproductive system is forced out. It is left behind in the body of the queen, and he dies.

After mating, the young queen returns to the hive, leaving her husband dead on the ground. The old queen then leads a swarm of workers, who fly away to start a new colony elsewhere. Honeybees

Mating flight of the queen honeybee pursued by drones. The queen
is larger than the worker or drones.

A swarm of honeybees. At the best time of the year this might contain between one and two thousand bees. They will stay like this for a few hours while the scouts look for a place to build a nest.

differ from all other social insects whose colonies reproduce by swarming, because it is the old queen who leads the swarm. Most of the workers that swarm with her are older than the ones left behind. Honeybees are valuable, and beekeepers do not usually let swarms escape. But sometimes you may see one, clustered on the branch of a tree, while scouts look round for a suitable place in which to build a nest.

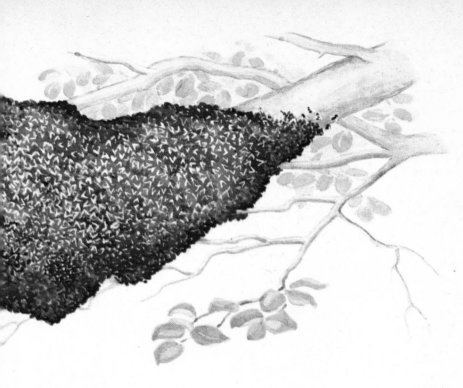

Before she settles down to her task of laying eggs, the new queen and her workers destroy all the rival grubs, pupae and newly emerged queens that have been fed on royal jelly. This is necessary because each colony can support only a single queen. Her presence regulates and maintains harmony in the hive. She produces a substance which the workers obtain by licking her. This "queen substance" is passed directly from one worker to another in re-gurgitated food. It enables all the other bees to know that their queen is present and in good health. It also prevents the reproductive organs, or ovaries, of the worker honeybees from developing. The spirit of the hive depends on the presence of a single, healthy queen.

Workers pushing a drone out of the hive.

At the end of summer, the remaining drones are driven out of the nest by the workers. They are seldom stung or killed, however, as has been claimed, but usually die from cold and hunger. Afterwards, the queen and her workers stay indoors, feeding on the honey and pollen that they have stored in the combs, until the warmth of spring again calls them out into the fields to collect nectar and pollen.

6
Bumblebees

Only about five percent of the known kinds of bees show any form of social life. The females of solitary species build simple nests and usually die before their offspring have even hatched from their eggs. In bumblebees, however, we find a degree of social life, but one that is much less well developed than in the honeybees.

Bumblebees are among our largest and most colorful insects. Unlike the colonies of honeybees, bumblebee colonies last only for a year. The story of a bumblebee colony begins in spring, for none but the fertilized queen survives the winter.

When she emerges from her hiding place, the queen is weak and drowsy. So she warms herself in

Bumblebee queen in early spring, having her first meal of nectar.

the sunshine before flying off to look for something to eat. At night, she hides under stones or fallen leaves until she has found a good place in which to build her nest.

Some kinds of bumblebees, known as "carder-bees," build their nests under grass tussocks, on the surface of the soil. Other kinds find holes underground. They often make their homes in the abandoned nests of shrews, field-mice or voles. Uninhabited birds' nests, bundles of hay and the thatched roofs of cottages are also sometimes used. These provide an abundance of dry grass and leaves with which the bumblebee can build her own nest.

When she has found a suitable place, the queen bumblebee pushes her way into the middle and hollows out a nesting chamber. She lines it with fine pieces of grass, moss and leaves. Occasionally, she flies out to look for food and brings back nectar. After she has built her first egg-cell, she arrives home with loads of pollen as well as nectar. This she empties from the "pollen baskets" on her back legs. The egg-cells are made of wax.

As in honeybees, there are glands which produce wax. These are on the upper and lower surfaces of the abdomen of the female bumblebee. With their hind legs, the bees take the scales of wax which issue from the ducts of these glands. Then they mould the wax in their jaws and use it to build egg-cells and honeycombs.

When the egg-cell is fully provisioned, the queen bumblebee lays a batch of eggs in it. Then she builds herself a honeypot of wax, just inside the entrance to her nest, and uses it to store nectar. She feeds on this when the weather is too cold and wet for her to go out foraging.

The tiny, newly hatched larvae are pearly white. They feed on the pollen which they find in the egg-cell. As they grow larger, the queen gnaws a hole in the roof of the egg-cell and feeds them on a mixture of honey and pollen. Every now and then she enlarges their cell with more wax. Eventually each grub spins a silken cocoon for herself, and becomes transformed into a pupa. The queen then removes the wax covering the cocoons, and uses it to build new egg-cells.

When her brood is developing, the queen bumblebee incubates the egg-cell with the heat from her own body. As the young workers emerge from their cocoons, they begin to carry out the various

Bumblebee queen of another species warming the first egg-cell with her body, the honeypot full of nectar beside her.

31

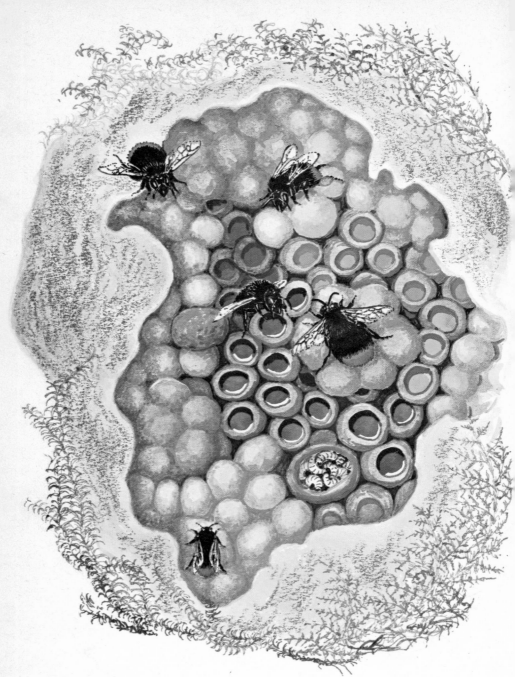

A section of a bumblebee nest showing brood cells covered with wax, old brood cells used as honeypots, cells filled with pollen and open brood cell containing larvae.

tasks which had previously been performed by the queen alone. A queen bumblebee never becomes just an egg-laying machine in the way that a queen honeybee does. Throughout her life she continues to help her workers to feed and incubate the brood.

During summer, male bumblebees are produced from unfertilized eggs and young queens are reared. As the older workers die off, the temperature of the nest is no longer regulated properly. Eventually, the young, impregnated queens disperse. They burrow into the ground, or seek some sheltered place in which to spend the winter. The old queen and the remaining workers and males then die, and the nest becomes completely derelict.

At the height of its activity, a nest of bumblebees may contain 300 or 400 workers. It is always much smaller than a colony of honeybees, and its social organization is less well-developed.

When the sun's rays first strike the nest, one of the workers can often be seen fanning her wings and making a loud hum. We now know that this fanning keeps the nest cool but, for many years, such bees were thought to be the "trumpeters" who woke the other bees and called them to work.

Before leaving the bumblebees, I must tell you about the cuckoo bumblebees that parasitize them. Cuckoos do not feed their young, but merely lay eggs in the nests of other kinds of birds. In the same way, cuckoo bumblebees lay their eggs in the nests of bumblebees, where they are reared by the workers of the colony.

33

Cuckoo bee (right) in nest of carder-bee (left).
The cuckoo bee is less hairy.

Cuckoo bumblebees do not collect nectar or pollen. There are no pollen baskets on their hind legs, and their stings are more powerful than those of bumblebees. Nevertheless, entry into a bumblebee nest is a dangerous process, and the cuckoo bee is quite often killed on her way in. Once established, however, she never leaves again.

Although the cuckoo bee does not kill the queen bumblebee, the colony produces no more adult bumblebees. So it is quite probable that cuckoo bees eat the eggs of bumblebees. The bumblebee colony dies out when there are no more workers left to forage. By this time, however, it will have reared several cuckoo bees to parasitize other bumblebee colonies in the neighborhood.

7
Social wasps

As in the case of the bees, only a few kinds of wasps are social. Most of them are sub-social or solitary. In temperate regions, the colonies of social wasps last only for a year, like those of bumblebees, but wasp colonies may persist for several years in the tropics.

Again, there are two kinds of females: egg-laying queens, and workers. Males appear for a short period at the end of the summer when they fertilize the young queens of the next generation. The workers are not quite sterile because some of them may lay eggs, especially if the queen dies. These unfertilized eggs produce only males, however, so that the workers alone could not carry on the colony.

Queen social wasp hibernating under bark.

The young queen hides away in hibernation during the winter. Sometimes you may find a queen wasp or hornet under a piece of bark, or hanging, motionless, throughout the winter behind a curtain. In the spring, she will fly away and start a new colony. She builds a small nest containing ten to twenty cells of "wasp paper," which she makes from chewed wood. (The use of wax by bees for making honeycombs is a great advance on the production of "wasp paper.") Scratches, made by the jaws of wasps, can be seen on almost any unpainted fence. The wood fibers are chewed up with saliva to make a paste that dries into grey or brownish "paper."

When the young worker wasps emerge from their cocoons, they take over the tasks of nest construction and feeding the developing grubs. Before long, the queen performs no duties other than laying eggs. Eventually she loses all powers of flight.

Social wasp workers scraping a wooden fence.

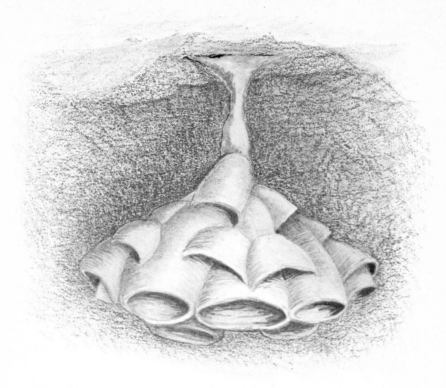

The first stages of the building of a wasp nest inside a hollow tree.

The nests of wasps and hornets begin as little pillars projecting downwards from the roof of an underground hole or inside a hollow tree. At the end of the pillar is built the first cell, to which others are added later. A dome-shaped envelope is then constructed over the cells and eventually covers the whole nest. A wasp colony in late summer may contain several thousands of cells and two or three thousand workers.

Although adult wasps feed on nectar, fruit juices and sweet things like jam, they feed their young on

A completed wasp nest in an attic, enveloped
in its covering of wasp "paper."

other insects such as flies or moths. These are
pounced on and chewed into "meat paste," but they
are not stung. After feeding the grubs, adult wasps
eagerly lick up a sweet secretion produced by special
glands associated with the mouth parts of the larvae.
Once again, the mutual exchange of food plays an
important part in regulating the life of the colony.

The wasp larva cannot foul the cell because its
crop does not communicate with the hind-gut until
the last stage of larval development.

8
Hunting-wasps and sand-wasps

Of all social insects, the wasps seem to have changed least from their solitary ancestors. Their colonies are never so highly organized as a beehive or an ants' nest. (All kinds of ants and termites are social.) The social wasps have not yet lost their primitive carnivorous habits, for they feed their larvae on "meat paste." In addition, they build their combs with "paper" composed of chewed fibers of wood. They have not developed the use of wax, as bees have.

Many kinds of wasps are quite solitary. Others are sub-social, showing only traces of true social behavior. Solitary hunting-wasps paralyze or kill

Hunting-wasp stinging her prey with the pointed ovipositor in her tail.

Sand-wasp dragging in her jaws a paralyzed caterpillar to the nest.

their prey with the help of the "ovipositor." This is the organ through which the eggs are laid. It can be modified to serve also as a sting. The prey can be a spider, a caterpillar, or some other insect. It is stored in the nest, and an egg is laid on it. When this hatches, the wasp larva feeds upon the paralyzed victim.

Nest-making, solitary wasps are of three kinds. The least advanced are spider-hunters. These first

catch and paralyze a spider. Then they hide it and look for a nesting site. This means that they only have to remember the position of the cell for a short time while they are dragging their prey to it.

Sand-wasps build their nests before they look for prey. This may be any kind of insect or spider. The nest consists of a long, branched tunnel. When several paralyzed creatures have been stored in it, an egg is laid and the cell is sealed up. The mother

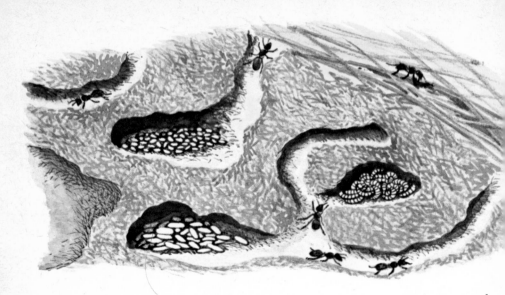

Section of an ant nest showing chambers with eggs, larvae and pupae, and workers looking after them.

has no contact with her young, but she constructs several nests in the same neighborhood, and has to remember where she has hidden them.

The most advanced of the solitary wasps do not bring food to the cells until the eggs have hatched. In this way the mother does look after her young to some extent, so she is called "sub-social." In certain African species, the female may feed her offspring with chewed fragments of prey, as social wasps do, instead of providing whole insects.

By studying the behavior of solitary wasps, we can discover the way in which true social behavior probably evolved. Colonies of social bees achieve a more advanced social structure than those of wasps do, but the most highly evolved social habits are found among ants and termites.

42

Queen's chamber of a termite colony, showing the queen in the center with the king on upper right, a pile of eggs, five workers on left and two kinds of soldiers.

Ants are more social than either bees or wasps, because they show a greater degree of specialization for various tasks. Not only are there queens, males and workers in the colony, but there may also be different kinds of soldiers, all of which are female. In termites, there are even more "castes" than among ants. Social insects are said to belong to different "castes" if they have become specialized for various purposes.

Among ants, there may be several castes of workers, which are, of course, all sterile females. In termites the distinction between castes is not related to sex. Termite workers and soldiers may be sterile females or sterile males, and there are several castes of reproductive termites, both winged and wingless.

9
Social insects and man

Man has been a social animal for about one million years. Social insects have existed for more than thirty times longer. The honeybee has been exploited by man since the beginning of our civilization. A cave painting at Araña, in Spain, gives a vivid impression of Palaeolithic man climbing down a rope-ladder to collect honey from a nest of wild bees on a rocky cliff.

Araña cave painting.

The honeybee is probably the most popular of all insects. Before the days of sugar, honey was about the only ingredient that could be used for sweetening food and drink. Bees' wax has long been used for polishing wood and for modeling figures. It has also been employed for over 2,000 years in the batik method of making designs on cloth. Only part of the cloth is dyed at a time, the rest being covered by removable wax. The work of bees is of importance, too, in the fertilization of fruit and agricultural crops. Other insects also do this, but only honeybees and bumblebees are equipped for collecting and carrying pollen from flowers of almost every shape and size.

Wasps of various kinds play an important part in controlling the numbers of insect pests. The benefits that they contribute probably outweigh the harm done to our fruit crops, for the fruit they attack is mainly overripe.

Bees and wasps can sometimes be troublesome because of their poisonous stings. These are modified ovipositors, as we have seen, so only queens and workers can sting. When a worker honeybee stings you, she dies. This is because her ovipositor is barbed and cannot be withdrawn. You have to pull it out yourself. Bumblebees do not lose their stings in that way and can, therefore, sting more than once.

Social wasps have stings with microscopic barbs which do not prevent them from being withdrawn after use. Larger kinds, such as hornets, are feared on account of their poison. Luckily, they tend to use their stings mainly in defense, especially of the nest. People are not often stung unless they disturb a nest, accidentally squash a wasp or bee, or take one into the mouth with fruit or jam.

Stings can be dangerous when they cause allergic reactions, so it is wise to be careful, but for most people the sting of a bee or wasp is nothing to worry about. Hornet stings are said to be very painful, but hornets are not nearly so ferocious as their appearance suggests, and they very seldom attack people.

The more one knows, the less there is to fear, and the less likely one is to make mistakes or get hurt. Now that you know more about bees and wasps, I hope you will enjoy watching them.

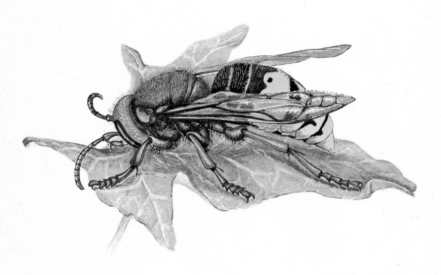

Hornet

Index

Ants, 7, 39, 42, 43

Bees, social, *see* Honeybees, Bumblebees; solitary, 19, 29
"Bee-bread," 15
Beehive, structure of, 9–10, 19; maintenance and protection of,
    13, 16
Brood cells in beehive, 9–10, 12, 19
Bumblebees, 19, 29–34, 45

"Carder-bees," 30, 34
Castes among social insects, 43
Colony, formation of, 24, 26, 29–30, 36; size of, 11, 33, 37; lifespan,
    29, 33, 34, 35, 36; *see also* Beehive, Nest, Temperature regulation
Communication between honeybees, 11, 27; *see also* Dancing
Cuckoo bumblebees, 33–4

Dancing of honeybees, 20–3
Defense of beehive or nest, 13, 34, 45–6
Drones (male honeybees), 24, 25, 28
Dung-beetles, 8–9

Egg-cells, (honeybees), 10, 12, 19; (bumblebees), 30–2; (wasps),
    36–7
Eggs, laying of, 9; (honeybees), 27; (bumblebees), 30–3; (wasps),
    35, 36

Food, (honeybees), 14, 15; *see also* "Royal jelly"; (bumblebees),
    30–1; (wasps), 37–8, 39
    gathering of, 14–16, 20–3, 30, 38
    sharing of, 11, 38
    storage of, 14, 15, 28, 30–1

"Gregarious" insects, 7
Grubs, *see* Larvae

Hibernation of queens, 33, 35, 36
Honey, 14, 15, 24, 28, 30–1; conversion from nectar, 16
Honeybees, 10–28, 44–5
Honeycomb, used for honey storage and egg cells, 10, 19; arrange-
    ment of, 19; advantage of, 36
Hornets, 36, 37, 45–6